D1161293

THE SCIENCE OF COLOR

INVESTIGATING THE COLOR

THE SCIENCE OF COLOR

INVESTIGATING THE COLOR

Adapted from Donna Bailey's
Investigating Red
by Barbara J. Behm

Gareth Stevens Publishing
MILWAUKEE

For a free color catalog describing Gareth Stevens's list of high-quality books, call 1-800-341-3569 (USA) or 1-800-461-9120 (Canada).

The editor would like to thank Anna Ciecka of the Department of Biological Sciences at the University of Wisconsin-Milwaukee for her assistance with the accuracy of the text.

Library of Congress Cataloging-in-Publication Data

Behm, Barbara J.
    Investigating the color red / adapted from Donna Bailey's
Investigating red by Barbara J. Behm. -- North American ed.
        p. cm. -- (The Science of color)
    Includes index.
    Summary: Investigates the color red and where it appears in our
world, finding it in flowers, in food, and in animals.
    ISBN 0-8368-1027-9
    1. Color--Juvenile literature. 2. Red--Juvenile literature.
[1. Red. 2. Color.] I. Bailey, Donna. Investigating red.
II. Title. III. Series: Science of color (Milwaukee, Wis.)
QC495.5.B446 1993   93-23817
535.6--dc20

North American edition first published in 1993 by
Gareth Stevens Publishing
1555 North RiverCenter Drive, Suite 201
Milwaukee, WI 53212, USA

This U.S. edition is abridged from *Investigating Red* © 1993 by Zoë Books Limited, Winchester, England; original text by Donna Bailey, © 1993. Additional end matter © 1993 by Gareth Stevens, Inc.

Photographic Acknowledgements
The publishers would like to acknowledge, with thanks, the following photographic sources:

Cover, Chris Newton/Frank Lane Picture Agency Ltd.; title, G. S. F. Picture Library; p. 6, Michael Jenner/Robert Harding Picture Library; p. 9, Agema Infrared Systems/Science Photo Library; p. 11, Trevor Hill; p. 15, Daphne Kinzler/Frank Lane Picture Agency Ltd.; p. 16 top, W. Broadhurst/Frank Lane Picture Agency Ltd.; p. 16 bottom, p. 17, Michael Holford; p. 18, G. S. F. Picture Library; p. 19 top, W. Wisniewski/Frank Lane Picture Agency Ltd.; p. 19 bottom, Ken Lucas/Planet Earth Pictures; p. 20, Chris Newton/Frank Lane Picture Agency; p. 21 top, Frank Lane Picture Agency Ltd.; p. 21 bottom, Peggy Heard/Frank Lane Picture Agency Ltd.; p. 22, Fritz Polking/Frank Lane Picture Agency Ltd.; p. 23, South American Pictures; p. 24 top, Sally and Richard Greenhill; p. 24 bottom, Robert Short/Robert Harding Picture Library; p. 25, R. G. Williamson/The Telegraph Colour Library; p. 26, Sally and Richard Greenhill; p. 27, Cliff Hollenbeck/Bruce Coleman Ltd.

Printed in the United States of America

1 2 3 4 5 6 7 8 9 99 98 97 96 95 94 93

CONTENTS

Words that appear in the glossary are printed in **boldface** type the first time they occur in the text.

THE SCIENCE OF RED

After it rains, a rainbow sometimes appears in the sky. Rainbows occur when light from the Sun is split into different colors by drops of rain.

Light may appear white, but it is actually made up of the seven colors of the **spectrum** – red, orange, yellow, green, blue, indigo, and violet.

To make a rainbow:

1. Put a glass of water on a sunny window ledge.
2. Place a sheet of white paper on the floor so that the Sun shines through the water and onto the paper.
3. Move the paper around until you see a rainbow.

Light

When you look at the ocean, you see waves. The distance from the top of one wave to the top of the next is a **wavelength**. Light travels in waves, too. Each color in the part of the spectrum we can see, known as the visible spectrum, has a different wavelength. Beyond both ends of this spectrum are invisible waves such as **X rays**, **microwaves**, and **infrared waves.**

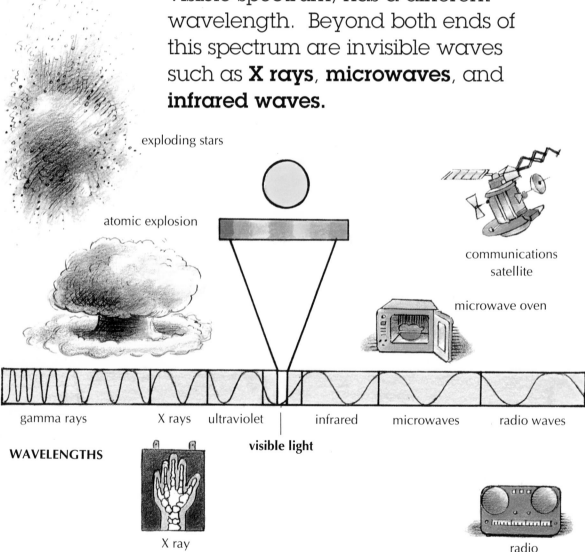

exploding stars

atomic explosion

communications satellite

microwave oven

gamma rays   X rays   ultraviolet   infrared   microwaves   radio waves

WAVELENGTHS

visible light

X ray

radio

Heat

We cannot see infrared waves, but we feel them as heat. A type of camera, called an infrared camera, is used to take photographs of things in the dark. This camera uses heat, not light, to take pictures. This is called **thermal imaging**. The photograph below was taken with an infrared camera to show where heat is escaping from the house.

Seeing light

People and other animals can see because our eyes are sensitive to light. The human eye contains a colored disk, called the **iris**. In the middle of the iris is a dark area called the **pupil**. Light enters the eye through the pupil. In bright light, the iris covers more of the pupil so that less light can enter the eye. In dim light, the iris covers less of the pupil so that more light can enter the eye. Images are upside-down when they reach the back part of the eye called the **retina**. The brain turns the images right side up again and "tells" us what we see.

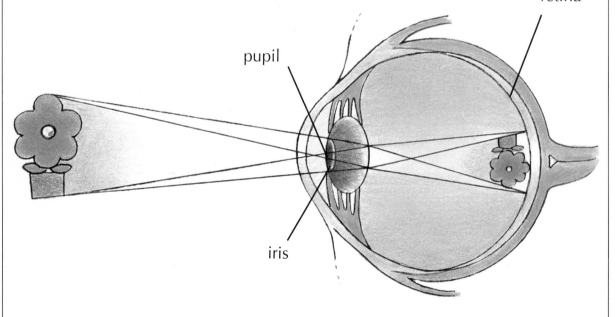

pupil

retina

iris

Seeing colors

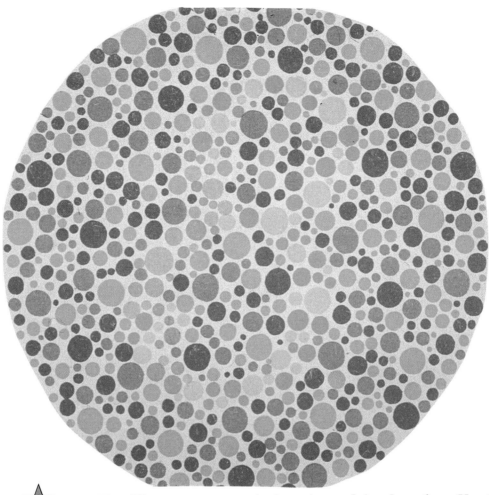

People who are color blind have a fault in the cones of their eyes. They cannot tell the difference between the colors red and green.

The eye contains two kinds of **cells** for seeing – rods and cones. Rods see only black and white. Cones see colors. There are three different kinds of cones. Red/yellow-sensitive cones absorb the longer wavelengths in the visible spectrum. Green-sensitive cones absorb wavelengths in the middle of the spectrum. Violet-sensitive cones absorb short wavelengths.

Mixing light

Red, green, and blue are called the **primary colors** of light. They cannot be made from any other colors. Together, they make white light. If you mix pairs of primary colors together, you get what are known as **secondary colors**: red and green make yellow; red and blue make magenta; and blue and green make cyan.

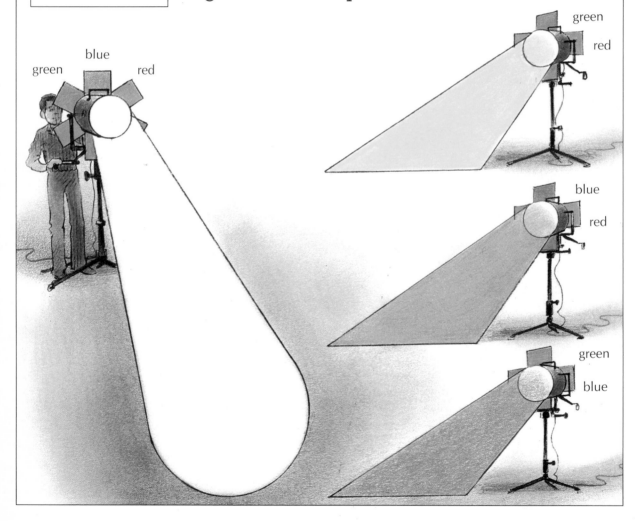

To make a rainbow spinner:

Draw a circle on some cardboard. Have an adult help you cut out the circle. Divide the circle into six segments, like a pie. Color each pair of opposite segments with one of the primary colors – red, green, and blue. Make a hole in one segment and a hole in the opposite segment. Thread a piece of string through the holes and tie it as pictured.

Wind up the spinner and pull the string tight to make the spinner whirl around. What happens to the colors?

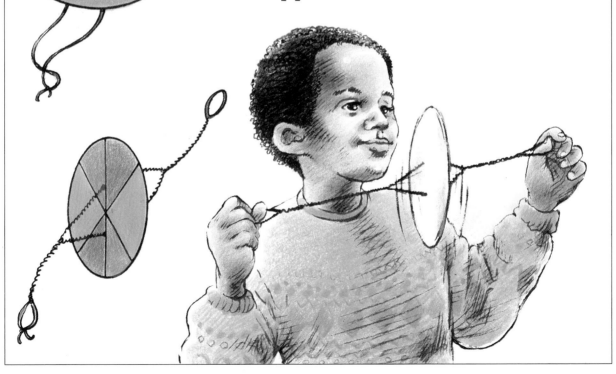

Mixing paint

When you mix paint, you do not get the same results as when you mix the colors of light. This is because paints and inks contain what are known as **pigments**. Pigments reflect the light of their own color and absorb the light of other colors. The primary colors of paint are red, yellow, and blue. Equal amounts of red and blue paint make a color called mauve; red and yellow paint make orange; blue and yellow paint make green; red, yellow, and blue paint make black.

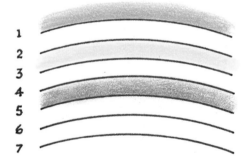

 To make a "paint" rainbow:
Draw seven arcs on a piece of paper. Number them 1 to 7. Paint arc 1 red. Paint arc 3 yellow. Paint arc 5 blue. Now experiment with those colors to get orange, green, indigo, and violet. Orange goes in arc 2, green in 4, indigo in 6, and violet in arc 7.

RED IN THE NATURAL WORLD

At sunrise and sunset, the sky near the Sun sometimes looks red. During those times, rays of light from the Sun must travel farther through the Earth's atmosphere than when the Sun is high in the sky. Most of the colors of light are scattered by dust and gas in the atmosphere. But red waves are undisturbed, making the sky look red.

In the earth

The soil in certain places looks red. This is because the ground there contains a **mineral** called iron ore. Crops usually grow well in this kind of soil.

Beautiful gemstones are also found in rocks and soil. Rubies are precious gems that are red in color. Garnets, shown in the picture below, are also red.

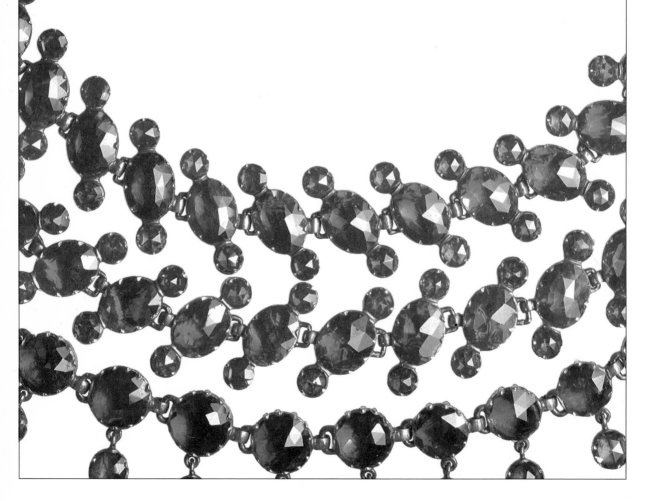

All around us

Terracotta is a brownish red clay that has been baked in an oven to make it hard. People in ancient Greece used terracotta to make statues, dishes, ornaments, buildings, and roads. This terracotta figure from Greece is over two thousand years old. Terracotta is still used today.

Many houses are built of red bricks made from clay. The bricks are red because of the iron ore in the clay.

Paints and dyes

A very long time ago, artists used iron ore to make red paint for their cave paintings. They also made red paint by grinding rocks that contained a mineral called cinnabar. The rock in the photograph contains cinnabar.

In ancient times, dyes were made from plants and the dried bodies of insects. Women used the root of the madder plant for lipstick. Today, the henna plant is still used to dye hair.

Attracting and warning

The male frigate bird above blows up the skin under its beak into a bright red bag to attract a female.

The reddish color of this arrow-poison frog warns birds and other small animals that the frog's skin is poisonous and can kill them.

Red flowers

A red flower reflects only red. The black center of a flower absorbs all the colors and does not reflect any, so we see it as black. A white flower reflects all the colors of light, and we see it as white.

These bright red poppies and other red flowers attract the attention of birds and butterflies that can easily see bright red colors. As the birds and butterflies move from flower to flower feeding on the flowers' nectar, they carry with them a fine dust called pollen. Flowers need pollen in order to produce seeds and fruits that will grow into new plants.

Red fruit

Birds and other animals are attracted by the red color of fruits such as strawberries and tomatoes.

In winter, bright red berries on certain plants attract birds. The birds eat the berries and swallow the seeds. Later, the seeds are passed out somewhere else in the birds' droppings. This spreads the plants over a large area.

Red birds

Flamingoes are large birds with long, red legs. Their feathers have black and red tips. The red on their legs and wings is from substances called **carotenoid** pigments found in the shrimp the flamingoes eat.

Red water

Some lakes and rivers look red because they contain red plants called **algae**.

The Red Sea, located between north-eastern Africa and the Arabian Peninsula, is so named for the red hills that surround it. The Red Sea is also colored by red seaweed, coral, and red animals and plants called **plankton**.

PEOPLE AND RED

People with red hair have the pigment **carotene** in their hair. We all have some carotene in our bodies. Our bodies change it into vitamin A.

Most people get red in the face when they exercise. Tiny **blood vessels** near the surface of the skin fill with blood. The extra heat built up from exercise escapes through the skin.

Blood

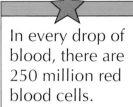

Exercise makes our hearts beat faster, sending more blood to our bodies. A substance called **hemoglobin** combines with oxygen to make blood red. Blood also carries heat to our bodies. These children getting exercise in the cold actually look warm because blood vessels near their skin make their faces look rosy.

Poor health

For some people, a red face or skin means poor health. Older people with red faces may have a heart problem. Red eyes may show that a person is tired or ill. When people have diseases such as chicken pox or measles, they get a rash of red spots on their skin. The young man below has measles.

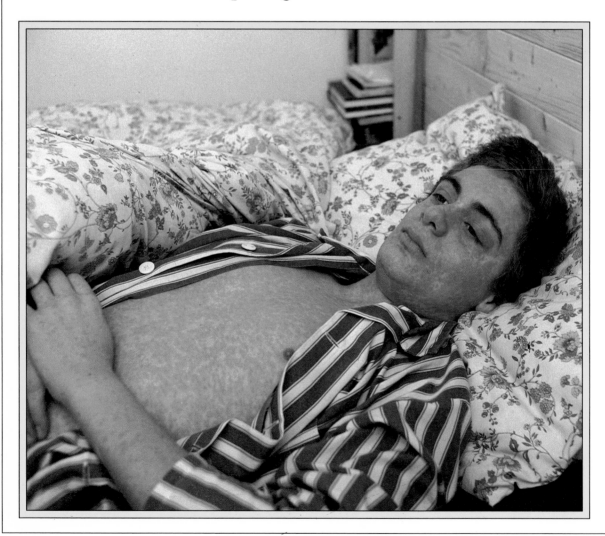

Danger

Humans, like other animals, use red to warn of danger or to attract attention. In many countries, drivers stop at red traffic lights. Some signs, such as the *STOP* sign, are red.

ACTIVITY
How many groups of words can you think of that contain the word *red*, such as *red alert* or *little red wagon*? See how many you can list.

GLOSSARY

algae: Very simple plants that grow in water and damp places.

blood vessels: Tubes in the body that carry blood to various parts of the body.

carotene: One of several kinds of red-yellow pigments that color various plants and animals.

carotenoid: Any of various red-yellow pigments found in plants and animals.

cells: The units that make up plants and animals.

complementary colors: Pairs of colored rays of light that, when mixed together, make white light.

hemoglobin: The substance in red blood cells that mixes with oxygen to make blood red.

infrared waves: Waves in the spectrum just beyond red waves. Infrared waves are felt as heat.

iris: The colored part of the eye.

microwaves: Waves in the spectrum between infrared and radio waves. Heat from microwaves is used in microwave ovens to cook food.

mineral:	A natural substance that has not been formed from plants or animals. Salt, rocks, and metals are all minerals.
pigment:	The coloring matter found in inks and paints.
plankton:	Tiny animals and plants that float on the surface of bodies of water.
primary colors:	The basic colors that cannot be made from any other colors.
pupil:	The dark area in the center of the eye through which light enters.
retina:	The area at the back of the eye that is sensitive to light.
secondary colors:	The colors made when two primary colors are mixed together.
spectrum:	The range of different wavelengths that includes the colors of light.
thermal imaging:	Photography that uses infrared heat waves.
wavelength:	The distance from the top of one wave to the top of the next.
X rays:	Powerful rays of light that pass through things that ordinary light cannot.

MORE BOOKS TO READ

Color and Light. Barbara Taylor (Franklin Watts)

Color and People. Marguerite Rush Lerner (Lerner)

Color: From Rainbows to Lasers. Franklyn M. Branley
(Harper Collins Children's Books)

Colors. Philip Yenawine (Delacorte)

The Invisible World of the Infrared. Jack R. White (Dodd,
Mead, & Company)

Of Colors and Things. Tana Hoban (Greenwillow)

Simple Science Projects with Color and Light. John
Williams (Gareth Stevens)

PLACES TO WRITE

Canadian Society for Color in Art, Industry, and Science
Institute for National Measurement Standards
NRC Ottawa, Ontario
K1A 0R6

Color Association of the United States
409 West 44th Street
New York, NY 10036

INDEX